ABRAHAM LINCOLN

A Photo-Illustrated Biography
by T.M. Usel

Historical Consultant
Steve Potts
Professor of History

Bridgestone Books

an Imprint of Capstone Press

jB
LINCOLN

Facts about Abraham Lincoln

- Abraham Lincoln went to school for less than a year.
- He studied law on his own and became a lawyer.
- He was elected to serve as the 16th president of the United States.
- He was shot and killed by John Wilkes Booth.

Bridgestone Books are published by Capstone Press • 818 North Willow Street, Mankato, Minnesota 56001
Copyright © 1996 by Capstone Press • All rights reserved • Printed in the United States of America

Library of Congress Cataloging-in-Publication Data
Usel, T.M.
    Abraham Lincoln, a photo-illustrated biography/T.M. Usel.
    p. cm.
    Includes bibliographical references (p. 24) and index.
    Summary: Presents the life story of the sixteenth president of the United States who is known for ending slavery in the U.S.
    ISBN 1-56065-341-8
    1. Lincoln, Abraham, 1809-1865--Juvenile literature. 2. Lincoln, Abraham, 1809-1865--Pictorial works--Juvenile literature. 3. Presidents--United States--Biography--Juvenile literature. 4. Presidents--United States--Pictorial works--Juvenile literature. [1. Linclon, Abraham, 1809-1865. 2. Presidents.] I. Title.
E457.905.U84 1996
973.7'092--dc20

95-42677
CIP
AC

Photo credits
Archive Photos: cover, 4-8, 12-18. The Lincoln Museum: 10, 20.

9.95

Table of Contents

Words in **boldface** type in the text are defined in the Words to Know section in the back of this book.

President of a Divided Nation

Abraham Lincoln was president during the Civil War (1861-1865). These were four of the hardest years in the history of the United States.

During the Civil War, the nation was divided. The North and the South were fighting about states' rights and slavery. Southerners thought they should be able to decide the issue of slavery for themselves. Northerners thought people should not own other people.

The end of the war brought an end to slavery. Abe Lincoln is remembered most for being the president who began to put an end to slavery.

He is famous for the Gettysburg Address. It starts "Four score and seven years ago, our fathers brought forth on this continent a new nation . . ." This is the speech he gave on November 19, 1863, at the cemetery in Gettysburg, Pennsylvania. Many soldiers were killed there during the Civil War.

Abraham Lincoln wore a tall stovepipe hat.

Young Man

Abe was born on February 12, 1809, near Hodgenville, Kentucky. His parents were Thomas and Nancy Lincoln.

Abe had less than a year of formal education, but he read as many books as he could find. He spent most of his time helping his father clear the land for farming. At the age of 19, Abe was hired to take cargo on a boat to New Orleans. He saw a black slave market for the first time.

When he was 22, Abe left home for New Salem, Illinois. He had several different jobs. His honesty in his dealings with people gave him the nickname Honest Abe.

He joined the town's **debate** team. Abe was becoming a good speaker and storyteller.

Politics interested Abe. In 1834, he was elected to the Illinois legislature as a **Whig.** He made his first public statement against slavery.

Lincoln and his father built a log cabin near Farmington, Illinois.

Marriage and Family

Abe decided to become a lawyer. There were no law schools then. Abe studied law books on his own and got his license to be a lawyer.

In 1837, Abe moved to Springfield, the capital of Illinois. He met Mary Todd, who was the daughter of a wealthy banker. Abe and Mary were married on November 4, 1842. Abe was 33, and Mary was 23.

During their marriage, Abe and Mary had four boys. Their names were Robert, Edward, William, and Thomas.

Abe was busy practicing law. In those days, judges and lawyers traveled from county to county. Court was held whenever they arrived in town. This was called traveling the circuit.

Abe got a lot of attention because he was so tall. He was six feet four inches (nearly two meters) tall.

Abe Lincoln married Mary Todd on November 4, 1842.

Powerful Lawyer

In 1846, Abe was elected to Congress as a representative from Illinois. He served one term and chose not to run for re-election. He returned to Springfield and practiced law again.

Many people were poor. They could not afford a lawyer. Often, Abe would give legal advice for free. He would even represent people in court for free.

Abe continued to travel the circuit. He handled many important cases. He was successful working for big businesses. Abe became one of the most powerful lawyers in Illinois.

Abe stayed out of politics for a while. But the issue of slavery brought him back. Abe and others were angered by lawmakers' actions in 1854 to leave the question of slavery up to the **territories**.

Abe Lincoln practiced law in Springfield, Illinois.

The Debates

In 1858, Abe ran for the U.S. Senate against Stephen Douglas. Douglas had sponsored legislation that allowed territories to decide whether to enter the United States as slave states or free states. This action by Congress would allow slavery to expand beyond the South.

Abe challenged Stephen Douglas to a series of seven debates. Many people came out to hear them in small Illinois towns.

Abe lost the election, but the debates made him famous. He received many invitations to give speeches. Many people who agreed with his stand against slavery wanted him to run for president.

In 1860, Abe ran for the nation's highest office as a member of the Republican Party. This was a new political party opposed to the expansion of slavery. He was elected to serve as the 16th president of the United States.

Stephen Douglas and Abe Lincoln were political rivals.

President of the United States

Shortly after Abe was elected president, South Carolina withdrew from the United States. Ten more southern states **seceded** from the Union, too, and formed the Confederacy. Many people from the South said they should be allowed to decide for themselves whether or not to allow slavery.

The Union and the Confederacy prepared for war. On April 12, 1861, Confederate soldiers fired shots at Union soldiers. This started the first battle of the Civil War at Fort Sumter in South Carolina.

Abe wanted to win the war to reunite the country. But he also wanted to make sure everyone was free. He wanted to put an end to slavery.

On January 1, 1863, Abe issued the Emancipation Proclamation. It freed all the slaves in the Confederacy. More than 3 million people were set free.

Abe signed the Emancipation Proclamation on January 1, 1863.

Second Term

The Civil War was still being fought when Abe ran for his second term as president. At the time, he was not very popular. Many people blamed him because their husbands, sons, and brothers had been killed in the war. Abe had even heard of a plot to kill him.

He knew there was a good chance that he would not be elected again. But he was a smart politician. Abe let the Union soldiers come home to vote for him. He was elected to a second term as president in November 1864.

The war ended on April 9, 1865. Soldiers returned home. Slavery was ended. The Union was back together again.

The Civil War was the bloodiest war in the history of the United States. More than 600,000 people were killed.

Abe ran for his second term as president during the Civil War.

Shot and Killed

On April 14, 1865, Abe went to a play at Ford's Theater in Washington, D.C. The play was a comedy called *Our American Cousin*.

During the play, a man named John Wilkes Booth opened the door at the back of the president's seating area. With a pistol, Booth shot Abe in the back of the head. Booth jumped to the stage and escaped.

A doctor had Abe moved to a building across the street. The doctor could not remove the bullet. Abe died the next morning. He was 56.

Abe's funeral was held at the White House on April 19. The next day, thousands of people stood in line to walk past the coffin.

On April 21, Abe's body was sent by train to Illinois. He was to be buried in Springfield. The train stopped in major cities along the way for thousands of people to pay their respects.

Abe's body was carried back to Springfield on a funeral train.

Remembering Lincoln

John Wilkes Booth was killed by government troops on April 26. Three other men and one woman were also caught. They were believed to be involved in a plot to kill the president and were hanged.

Abe was not always popular while he was president. He was elected to the office with less than 40 percent of the total vote. Yet, many consider him to be one of the best presidents the United States has ever had.

Abe had great inner strength. When he believed in something, he could persuade many other people to believe in it, too.

He will always be remembered for helping free the slaves and for bringing the country together again after a war.

Many people think Abe was one of the best presidents ever.

Words from Abraham Lincoln

"My paramount object in this struggle is to save the Union, and is not either to save or destroy slavery. If I could save the Union without freeing *any* slave, I would do it, and if I could save it by freeing *all* the slaves I would do it; and if I could save it by freeing some and leaving others alone I would also do that."

From a letter Lincoln wrote to Horace Greeley, the editor of the *New York Tribune*, August 22, 1862. As the war progressed, Lincoln's goal changed. He wanted to win the war so everyone would be free.

"If my name ever goes into history, it will be for this act, and my whole soul is in it."

After issuing the Emancipation Proclamation on January 1, 1863.

Important Dates in Abraham Lincoln's Life

1809 – Born on February 12 in Kentucky

1828 – First sees the slave market in New Orleans

1830 – Lincoln family moves to central Illinois

1834 – Elected to Illinois legislature

1842 – Marries Mary Todd

1846 – Elected to the U.S. Congress

1858 – Lincoln-Douglas debates

1860 – Elected as president of the United States

1861 – Civil War begins

1863 – Issues Emancipation Proclamation

1863 – Gives Gettysburg Address

1864 – Elected for a second term as president

1865 – Civil War ends; Booth kills Lincoln

Words to Know

debate—to discuss both sides of an issue

politics—the art or science of governing

seceded—formally withdrew from the United States

territories—places that were part of the United States with their own legislatures and appointed governors, but without the status of states

Whig—political party that existed from 1834 to 1856. Most northern Whigs became Republicans and most southern Whigs became Democrats.

Read More

Clark, Philip. *Abraham Lincoln.* East Sussex, England: Wayland, 1981.

Freedman, Russell. *Lincoln: A Photobiography.* New York: Clarion Books, 1987.

Gross, Ruth Belov. *True Stories About Abraham Lincoln.* New York: Lothrop, Lee & Shepard, 1973.

McNeer, May. *America's Abraham Lincoln.* Lakeville, Conn.: Grey Castle Press, 1991.

Useful Addresses

Abraham Lincoln Association
Old State Capitol
Springfield, IL 62701

Friends of the Lincoln Museum
c/o Abraham Lincoln Museum
Lincoln Memorial University
Harrogate, TN 37752

Center for the Study of the Presidency
208 East 75th Street
New York, NY 10021

Lincoln Heritage Trail Foundation
P.O. Box 1507
Springfield, IL 62705

Index